STUMPED FOR A TALE?

Stumped for a Tale?

CRICKET STORIES FROM THE STARS

Collected by Brian Johnston

'THE CRICKETER' WITH STANLEY PAUL
London

STANLEY PAUL & CO LTD
178–202 Great Portland Street, London W1

AN IMPRINT OF THE  HUTCHINSON GROUP

London Melbourne Sydney
Auckland Bombay Toronto
Johannesburg New York

★

First published by THE CRICKETER 1965
This new and revised edition 1966

This book has been set in Times, printed in Great Britain
on Antique Wove paper by Anchor Press and
bound by Wm. Brendon, both of Tiptree, Essex

Introduction

A FEW YEARS ago my old friend and colleague, the late Roy Webber, and I had the idea of making a collection of amusing cricket stories and of putting them together in a book. We had had so many laughs during our travels round the grounds in the summer and at cricket dinners in the winter that we thought it a pity not to "share the joke."

We therefore had the audacity and cheek to write to many of our cricketing friends—either famous players or well-known personalities—who happened to love cricket. We asked each one to send us his own particular favourite story and were very surprised and gratified at the response. One or two, I admit, said we were trying to get something for nothing (we were)—a few thought we were spoiling the market for after-dinner speakers. But this book is not intended as a glossary or reference book. Its only intention is to amuse.

Some of the stories are chestnuts but in my view not necessarily the worse for that; others are new to me and I hope new to you too. I should like to thank all our friends who sent us their stories and to apologise to those who find that theirs has not caught the selector's eye! In most cases this was because of duplication and I fear that they lost the toss!

BRIAN JOHNSTON

From: M. J. K. SMITH, Warwickshire and England.

WHEN he was up at Oxford, Jon (Pom-Pom) Fellows-Smith used to have his leg pulled unmercifully by Jumbo Jowett. One day Pom-Pom was sitting writing letters in the dressing-room in the Parks. This is at the back of the pavilion and is underground so that it is impossible to watch the game from it. Jumbo rushed in and said, " You are in, Pom-Pom." Pom-Pom picked up his batting gloves and bat and walked out, and as was usual with him, kept his eyes fixed on the ground with his bat trailing behind him. When he had got about half way to the wicket he heard roars of laughter from the crowd. Looking up he saw that the game was going on in the middle and that no-one was out. He returned to the pavilion threatening to " fill Jumbo in."

In the next match v. Middlesex, he was again writing letters in the dressing-room when a young chap being tried for the University went in to bat. Pom-Pom was the next man in. After about two minutes Jumbo Jowett again rushed in and said, " Lawrence is out, you are in, Pom-Pom," but this time Pom-Pom refused to believe him and went on writing letters. He wasn't going to be caught twice! However, a few moments later Lawrence came into the dressing-room and began taking off his pads, so Pom-Pom realised that this time his leg had *not* been pulled. He picked up his batting gloves and again rushed out to the wicket. But still determined not to be caught out a second time he looked up as he walked, and to his surprise he saw that there was no-one on the field except the two umpires. J. J. Warr, who was captaining the Middlesex team, had been let into the joke and had taken all his team and hidden them behind the sightscreen!

What Pom-Pom said cannot be printed in this book.

From: WILFRED RHODES, Yorkshire and England.

A SOUTHERNER who was staying in Leeds decided to watch the annual Roses Match between Yorkshire and Lancashire. Before the game started he found a seat and went off to get a drink—placing his hat neatly on the seat where he had been sitting. On returning a few minutes later he found that his hat had been removed to the floor, and a large Yorkshireman was sitting on his seat. Somewhat diffidently he said, "Excuse me, Sir, I think you are sitting on my seat, I reserved it with my hat." The Yorkshireman replied, " I'm sorry, lad, it's bums what keep seats up 'ere, not 'ats."

From: FRED TITMUS, Middlesex and England.

O NCE when Middlesex had to follow on due to some very bad batting, one of the Middlesex batsmen in the dressing-room called out to John Warr, "What's the order in the second innings, Skipper?" Warr replied, "Same order—different batting."

From: PETER WEST, television commentator.

I ONCE asked George Hirst if he thought anyone would ever beat his record of 2,000 runs and 200 wickets in a season—which he performed in 1906. "Ah doan't know," said George, " but I do know one thing, if anyone ever does, he'll be mighty tired."

JOHN PAWLE, the racquets player who got a cricket Blue for Cambridge in 1936 and 1937, tells a delightful story about his late father.

MY father was very absent-minded and also rather fierce, so that everyone was slightly scared of him. He used to run his own cricket team which played on his lovely ground in the village of Widford. On one occasion the visiting side batted first and my father put on a fast bowler to open the bowling. It was a very hot day and after an hour this fast bowler was still bowling and becoming hotter and hotter, and slower and slower. Another half hour went by and there was still no change of bowling, and the poor chap was in a pitiable state. At last after a short conference with the rest of the side, one of its senior members plucked up courage and approached my father. "Don't you think old Brown is getting a little bit tired, sir?" "Yes, I quite agree," came the reply, "I can't see why they don't take him off."

From: JOHN ARLOTT

HE was a very slow bowler and had been hit more or less out of sight when at length the batsman missed a ball which pitched straight—like the others it was devoid of spin—and struck him on the pad. The bowler turned round with a howl of triumph to the umpire and cried "How's that?"

"Not out," said the umpire. The bowler was a very well-bred cricketer and it was not until the end of the over, when he had been hit for three more sixes, that he said to the umpire:

"That one pitched straight, didn't it?"

"Yes."

"It didn't turn did it?"

"No."

"He didn't touch it, did he?"

"No."

"Then why wasn't he out?"

"It wasn't going fast enough to disturb the bails!"

HAROLD LARWOOD was once staying with a friend in the West Country, and visited a village cricket match on the Saturday afternoon. The visiting side were one short and Larwood was pressed to play without anyone knowing who he was. As both umpires came from the home side, who were batting, it proved difficult to get them out. In desperation the Captain asked Larwood if he could bowl. He said that he would have a try and, taking a short run, sent down an off-spinner, which the batsman missed and hit him in the middle of both legs which were right in front of the wicket. To the appeal—"Not out" was the reply. The next one, a leg break, was snicked into the wicket-keeper's hands. Again "Not out" was the reply. Larwood then took his usual run of over 20 yards and sent down a thunderbolt which knocked all three stumps out of the ground. Turning to the umpire he said, "We very nearly had him that time, didn't we?"

ONCE when Sir Pelham was captain of Middlesex they were playing Surrey at the Oval. On the last day Surrey only needed a few runs to win with plenty of time and wickets in hand. So Sir Pelham put himself on to bowl and by some fluke got a ball through Andy Sandham's defence. It rapped him on the pads but Sir Pelham's confident appeal was turned down by the umpire. Surrey won shortly afterwards, and as the players walked off the field, Sir Pelham, as courteous and polite as ever, said to the umpire: "You know I never dream of questioning an umpire's decision. But just as a matter of interest, why did you turn down my appeal for l.b.w.?" "Well, sir, you see," said the umpire, "one half of the ball would have missed the stumps!"

From: JACK TRAIN, broadcaster and comedian

ONE day in a match between the village and a team got together by the local peer, his lordship's butler was pressed into service as umpire.

When his lordship batted he had the misfortune to be called for too short a single by his partner, and easily failed to make his ground before the wicket was broken.

There was a triumphant appeal from the village side and all eyes turned on the butler, who was faced with such an appalling decision to make. He drew himself up and with tremendous dignity said: "His lordship is not in."

From: FRED BEATTIE, Lancashire Committee

WHEN wickets are falling it's not always easy to decide whether it's due to good bowling or weak batting. Someone is clean bowled. Was it a good ball or a poor stroke? A perfect answer to this problem was given to me by Winston Place. When going in first for Lancashire he had his off-stump removed first ball. On returning to the pavilion a sympathetic member said to him as he passed: "Bad luck, Winston. That was a good ball." "Yes, it was," replied Winston, "the way I played it."

From: BRIAN JOHNSTON

WHILST his side was fielding, one man appealed all day for almost everything from the square leg position where he was fielding. When it was his turn to bat and he asked for guard, the umpire said to him: "Where would you like me to give it from—here or square leg?"

From: G. C. NEWMAN, President of Middlesex

THIS is a story about that lovable character Jim Sims. Nigel Haig had sent him in to open the Middlesex innings against Nottinghamshire in the heyday of Larwood and Voce. Jim faced this terrifying ordeal with "a certain amount of apprehension," and although he managed to stay there and accumulate a few runs by snicks and edges, he was battered and bruised all over his body. When I joined him at the fall of a wicket, Jim called out in a confidential whisper from behind his hand, "MR. NEWMAN, here a minute." Thinking I was about to receive some useful advice about how to play the fast bowling, I went up to him and said, "Yes, Jim. What is it?" "It's toffee!" said Jim, and walked away.

From: G. O. ALLEN, Middlesex and England

IN 1921 Eton were beaten by Winchester by a large margin in the annual school match. The Eton Captain was W. W. Hill-Wood—a very good batsman and a useful leg-break bowler. After the game he asked George Hirst, who was then coach at Eton, why they had lost. The reply was short and to the point, "You bowled too much and too bad!"

From: BRIAN JOHNSTON

WHILST with the last M.C.C. team in Australia poor David Sheppard came in for more than his fair share of dropped catches. The story was going around that a young English couple who had settled in Australia were due to have their first-born christened. The husband suggested that it would be nice if they got David Sheppard to do it for them. "Oh no," said the horrified wife, "not likely, he would only drop it!"

WITHOUT being too immodest I made a particularly good stumping on the leg-side when playing in an up-country match on one of my tours of Australia. As I whipped off the bails I shouted to the umpire, "How's that?", and the umpire replied, "Bloody marvellous!"

From: ERNEST EYTLE, cricket commentator

A story is told of the West Indies team who came to England in a banana boat for their tour of 1957. A certain member of the team was said not to be able to write very well and it was essential to teach him at least to write his own autograph in view of the numerous demands always made on touring teams. Everton Weekes volunteered to teach him and each day he took his pupil to his cabin for his lesson. At the end of the voyage the Manager asked Everton how his pupil had got on and Everton said, "Very well," and produced a thousand autographs as proof.

To his horror, the Manager saw that each autograph read "Everton Weekes"! A cunning way of Everton saving himself from getting writer's cramp!

From: The late ROY WEBBER

THERE is always the ever-present danger for a commentator of saying the wrong thing by mistake. In 1961 Brian Johnston committed the gaffe of all time. The B.B.C. were televising the Third Test at Leeds and the camera swung round to show Neil Harvey standing very close in at leg-slip. Without thinking Brian said, "That's Neil Harvey there, standing with his legs wide apart, waiting for a tickle!"

Jack Fingleton did not make matters any better by butting in—"I beg your pardon, *what* did you say? I hope you mean waiting for a catch." Needless to say, Brian did not dare answer—in fact he was speechless for a few minutes, probably much to the delight of the cricket experts!

From: DENIS COMPTON, Middlesex and England

IN a Middlesex match at Lord's before the war R. W. V. Robins had just completed a very productive over as far as the batsmen were concerned, and decided that it was time to make a change. He called over to Jim Smith, the Middlesex fast bowler, "Take the next over at this end, Jim." Umpire Bill Reeves walked across to Robins and said, " Do you want your sweater, Sir?" As it was a hot and perspiring day, Robins rather grumpily said to Reeves, " Keep the b . . . . sweater; and you know what you can do with it."

"What, Sir?" said Reeves, " swords and all ! "

From: GEORGE COX, Sussex

YORKSHIRE were playing Somerset in the good old days. Emmott Robinson was bowling when in came the next batsman; a real gentleman, I Zingari, bristling moustache, silk shirt ("Never wore a vest in my life!"), spotless batting trousers, well-whitened pads and boots, and a highly-coloured fancy cap. "Good morning, Robinson," he said on his way to the wicket. Emmott took an immediate dislike to him. The batsman arrived at the wicket, took guard, and then took ages looking round the field, walking or strutting around as he did so. At last the batsman was ready, and Emmott bowled him a snorter, pitching on the leg stump and hitting the top of the off. On his way out he said, "Well bowled, Robinson, it was a fine ball."

And Emmott replied, "Aye, but t'were wasted on thee."

From: The late E. R. T. HOLMES, Surrey and England

BILL REEVES, the famous umpire, was seldom at a loss for a reply. But he was struck dumb on one occasion as follows: Surrey were playing Gloucester at Cheltenham, and Alf Gover, Surrey's traditional number eleven, strode to the crease. He took up his stance ready to withstand the onslaught, scorning to take guard. Bill Reeves was never surprised at anything, but noting this somewhat irregular behaviour on Gover's part said, "Hey, Alf, don't you want your guard?"

"No thanks," said Alf, "I've played here before."

From: SIR STANLEY ROUS, President of F.I.F.A.

A few years ago I was trying to arrange a programme for some Swiss visitors to this country, and asked them if they would like to see some Test cricket. They replied, "No, we would much rather see the real thing."

From: The late ARTHUR WRIGLEY, the cricket statistician

A N old lady was once told that Laker had taken three wickets for four—she said it was a pity he was so short-sighted.

The same lady heard a commentator say that May had been dropped when he was two—and remarked that mothers should be more careful with their babies.

The same lady when hearing, in a commentary, that Jim Laker had only got one short leg, wrote and asked—" Was it an accident, or was he born that way?"

A witch doctor in Tanganyika was ill for some time and came to England to see a specialist. Whilst here he thought he would see whether the magic in England was better than the magic in his own country. On returning home he was asked by another witch doctor if he had seen any examples of white magic. "Yes," he said, "I did. One day I went to a big sports stadium where thousands of people had assembled and were sitting in brilliant sunshine. The grass was beautiful and the grandstands were white and gleaming with new paint. I had been sitting there for half-an-hour enjoying the warm sun, when a man came out of a hut—went to the middle of the grass and put three pieces of wood upright into the ground. He then walked a measured distance and put in three more pieces of wood.

I then enjoyed the sun for another half hour. And then two men in white coats came out of the hut, walked to the middle of the grass and put some smaller pieces of wood on top of the other six pieces. Then eleven men came out of the hut and spread themselves around the field, and one of them had protective pads on his legs, and big gloves on his hands. A minute or two later two more men came out of the hut, also wearing gloves and pads and carrying pieces of timber. Each went and stood against the three pieces of wood in the ground. Then one of the men in white coats threw a red ball to one of the men in the field. He walked twenty yards away and when he was by himself he began to rub the ball—first on his shirt—and then on his trousers. As soon as he did that it began to pour with rain and it went on raining for five hours. What wonderful magic."

From: KEN BARRINGTON, Surrey and England

DURING the tour of India in 1961/62, the M.C.C. had arrived for an up-country game and they were staying in a prince's palace. There was nothing very much to do and I asked one of the bearers if there was a snooker table we could use. The bearer did not understand what I was saying so I went through the actions which I thought would illustrate it. Suddenly he smiled and went running out of the room. Five minutes later he came back with a flit gun.

Another from KEN BARRINGTON

ON another occasion I left Bombay after having tummy trouble and arrived in an up-country town having been told by the doctors to eat one coconut a day. So I asked the bearer for a coconut but had some difficulty in making him understand what I wanted. Eventually it appeared that he had got the drift and on his return brought a tray on which was a plate of nuts and a coca-cola.

From: FRANK WOOLLEY, Kent and England

WHEN playing at Queenstown in South Africa in the 1909–10 Tour I was bowling for M.C.C. with Strudwick keeping wicket. The batsman ran six yards down the wicket—missed the ball—and Struddy whipped off the bails. The batsman looked round—fell full length—and pushed his bat into the crease. Struddy appealed and the man stood up—brushed himself down as the umpire said "Not out!" This was too much for even such a good sportsman as Struddy who politely asked the umpire, "Why did you give the batsman 'Not out'?"

"Oh," said the umpire, "he was back before you appealed."

From: JOHN WARNER

JUST after the war I went to live at a small village in Hertfordshire and was invited to play on the home ground in the first match, beginning at 2.30.

My wife said she would come down about 3.0 and when she duly arrived at this hour was surprised to find us—though it was a lovely day—standing by the pavilion with no cricket in progress. "You are very late starting," she said, to which I had to reply: "Nonsense! We have already batted and are out for nine!!" When we fielded the other side were very pushed to win by one wicket.

The sequel to this match in which I made nought, and the next one in which I made one, came in the third home match. When going in number four I received four balls, from the first one of which four came from the edge of the bat, from the second two from a mishit over short-leg, and from the third (the last ball of the over) a single, which in truth was a leg-bye.

The first ball of the next over demolished my wicket and as I reached the pavilion, having made seven, our village fast bowler walked up to me wreathed in smiles, extended his hand and with great sincerity said: "It's splendid, Mr. Warner, to see that you have run into form!"

This fine innings was in fact easily top score.

From: DESMOND EAGAR, Secretary of Hampshire

WHEN he landed in Jamaica for his private cricket tour, the Duke of Norfolk was presented with a bouquet by a little girl who had been told: "When you address the Duke do not forget to say 'Your Grace.'"

She duly presented the flowers with a charming "For what we are about to receive may the Lord make us duly thank-ful!"

From: F. R. BROWN, Northants and England

DURING the Fourth Test Match at Adelaide of the 1950–51 M.C.C. Tour of Australia, I had the misfortune one night to run into a street lamp standard in my car. The car was wrecked but luckily I escaped comparatively uninjured. When batting in the Fifth Test soon after at Melbourne, Ray Lindwall bowled me a very fast ball wide of the off-stump, at which I had a terrific swish and missed by a mile. A voice from the crowd promptly shouted, "I say, Brownie, it's a pity you didn't miss that Adelaide lamp standard by as much as you missed that ball!"

From: The late GILBERT HARDING

A visiting non-Catholic cricket team was playing against a Roman Catholic School. One of the visiting batsmen was well on his way to a century. He hit a boundary off the first ball, two runs off the second, a boundary off the third, and was waiting to receive the fourth ball when the Abbey Church bells began to ring the Angelus. Caps came off, the field assumed a prayerful attitude and everyone made the sign of the cross. Never in his life had the batsman seen this happen, and it shook him so much that the fourth ball clean bowled him middle stump. Back in the pavilion, the batsman still dazed by what had happened said, "I've been bowled out, caught out and run out, but never before have I been prayed out."

From: JOHN ELLISON, broadcaster

IN a village match a visiting batsman was hit high on the chest by the local fast bowler—the village blacksmith.

To his surprise the bowler appealed for l.b.w., and to his even greater surprise the umpire gave him out. As he passed the umpire on his way back to the pavilion, the batsman said, "I couldn't possibly have been out, it hit me in the chest."

"Well," said the umpire, "you look in the local *Gazette* next Thursday, and you'll see you were out right enough."

"*You* look," snorted the batsman, "I am the Editor!"

* * * * *

W. G. GRACE was batting on a very windy day, and a fast bowler succeeded in getting one past him which just flicked the bails off. The Doctor stood his ground and said to the umpire, "Windy day today, umpire."

Whereupon the umpire replied, "Very windy indeed, Doctor—mind it doesn't blow your cap off on the way back to the pavilion!"

ANOTHER story about Bill Reeves. A young amateur playing for the first time for Lancashire was the most immaculate thing ever seen outside Savile Row. New pads, glistening white shirt and flannels, gaudy club cap. As he went in to bat it started to drizzle. First ball there was an appeal for l.b.w. against him. " Out," says Reeves. During lunch the young amateur went up to Reeves, and said, "I don't think I was out, Mr. Reeves."

"No, you weren't," said Reeves and walked off. The young man fretted all the rest of the day and at close of play went up to Reeves again. " Mr. Reeves, excuse me, but I have been thinking about what you said at lunch time. If you think I wasn't out, why on earth did you give me out?"

" Well, sonny, I was thinking of your poor old Mother—whatever would she have done if you had caught your death of cold?"

From: DENIS COMPTON

ON the second day of the New Zealand Test Match at the Oval in 1949 I was held up in a traffic block at Marble Arch a few minutes after 11.00 a.m. The chap in the next car glanced across with an expression of horror on his face, and said, "But, shouldn't you be at the Oval?"

"Yes," I said, "I am on my way now."

"But you ought to be there," said the motorist, turning up the car radio. "It's an 11 o'clock start." And to my consternation, I heard the commentator say, "Denis Compton is the next batsman and he will be coming down the steps any moment now."

... Just how wrong can a commentator be?

From: CLIFFORD MOLLISON, the actor

WHENEVER I arrive late at Lord's for an important match I'm so keen to see what the score is that I usually run up the steps of "O" block and watch play from the back of the stand, rather than waste time going round to the Pavilion. I did this at one Test Match before the war and had been watching for about five minutes when I became conscious of some heavy breathing behind me and the sort of mixed odour of beer and spirits which you get on entering any pub. I looked round and saw a large elderly gentleman a little bit the worse for wear, with a stained drooping moustache and wearing an old-fashioned palm beach suit and a Panama hat on his head.

"Who's bowling?" he asked gruffly.

"Verity, Sir."

"Bloody fools. Why don't they put Hammond on?"

During the next over he asked the same question. This time I replied: "Farnes, Sir."

"Bloody fools. Why don't they put Hammond on?"

This same routine went on whenever there was a change of bowling. At last, later in the day, Hammond was put on and believe it or not his first three balls were hit for 4, 4, and 6.

"Who's bowling now?" my friend asked.

"Hammond, Sir," I replied.

"Bloody fools. What can they expect if they keep a chap hanging about in the slips all afternoon?"

And so saying he shuffled off.

WHEN he was at school Gilbert Harding hated cricket. The headmaster, appreciating this, excused him playing on condition that he took some other exercise such as walking or tennis. But the games master was always very annoyed about this and got his own back one day (so he thought) by making Gilbert Harding umpire in the annual match of the Masters v. The Boys. The Masters batted first and the games master, resplendent in his Oxford Authentic cap, batted superbly and was 99 not out when a bowler from the end at which Gilbert Harding was umpiring hit him high up on the left thigh. "How's that?" said the bowler.

"Out," said Gilbert. The games master was furious and as he passed Gilbert on his way back to the pavilion said, "Harding, you weren't paying attention. I wasn't out."

Gilbert replied, "On the contrary, I *was* paying attention and you weren't out!"

DURING the 1962 Lord's Taverners v. Old England match Norman Wisdom was playing for the Lord's Taverners and had the 15,000 crowd roaring with laughter at his antics at the crease whilst he was batting. In the pavilion an elderly M.C.C. member in a panama hat with I Z. ribbon was watching the whole proceedings in a slight daze, obviously not quite realising what was going on out in the middle. After a time Norman did one of his famous mock falls as he collided with his fellow batsman in mid-pitch and the crowd roared their approval. The elderly member chuckled and nudged his neighbour and said, "That man ought to be a comedian."

One about GEORGE GEARY, Leicestershire and England

A RAW young amateur was captaining Leicester in the thirties when E. W. Dawson could not play. In those days, of course, it was more or less unheard of for the senior professional to be allowed to captain. The opposition batted and had made well over 300 by 6 o'clock with very few wickets down. Not once had the young amateur consulted George about his bowling changes but finally in desperation he did go up to him and ask who he thought ought to go on. "Put the clock on," said George, "and then we can all go home!"

From: BRIAN JOHNSTON

WE commentators are in a spot of "maiden" trouble. Only the other week a listener wrote to the *Radio Times* and reminded us of an occasion when Rex Alston was commentating on a Middlesex match a few years ago.

Jack Young was bowling over after over with his usual accuracy and at the end of one of them Rex remarked: "Well, that's the end of another Young maiden!"

And now, after the Leeds Test, I have received a puzzled letter from a lady viewer. She had switched on her set and heard me say: "That's two maidens running from Trueman." This reminds me of one of the best commentators' slips in recent years. It was during an interval between innings and the commentator, who shall be nameless, said: "The ground staff are coming on to roll the pitch and they are pushing the medium pace roller!"

From: NAUNTON WAYNE, the actor

BEFORE the start of a needle village match, the home Captain found he was one short. In desperation he was looking round the ground for someone he could rope in to play when he spotted an old horse grazing quietly in the field next door. So he went up to him and asked him if he would like to make up the side. The horse stopped eating and said: "Well, I haven't played for some time and am a bit out of practice but if you're pushed, I'll certainly help you out," and so saying jumped over the fence and sat down in a deck-chair in front of the pavilion. The visitors lost the toss and the home side batted first, the horse being put in last. They were soon 23 for 9 and the horse made his way to the wicket wearing those sort of leather shoes horses have on when they are pulling a roller or a mower. He soon showed his eye was well in and hit the bowling all over the field. When he wasn't hitting sixes he was galloping for quick singles and never once said "Neigh" when his partner called him for a run. Finally he was out hoof before wicket for a brilliant 68, and the home side had made 99.

When the visitors batted the home Captain put the horse in the deep and he saved many runs by galloping round the boundary and hoofing the ball back to the wicket-keeper. However the visitors were not losing any wickets and were soon 50 for 0. The home Captain had tried all his regular bowlers in vain when he suddenly thought of the horse. He had batted brilliantly and now was fielding better than anyone. At least he could do no worse than the other bowlers. So he called out do him: "Horse, would you like to take the next over at the vicarage end?" But the horse was terribly annoyed. "You silly fool," he shouted back, "whoever heard of a horse who could BOWL?"

From: The late R. C. ROBERTSON-GLASGOW, Somerset

IN a village cricket match a very fat batsman came in to bat, and as he was taking up his stance at the wicket the local umpire confided to the visiting bowler: "We have a special rule for him. If you hit him in front it's l.b.w., if you hit him behind it's a wide!"

From: NORMAN YARDLEY, Yorkshire and England

EACH year at the beginning of the season Yorkshire play, or used to play, some one-day matches against clubs around the county. The idea was to give the team some practice out in the middle before starting their championship matches. One year they were playing against a club just outside York. Yorkshire fielded first and Freddie Trueman soon got among the wickets, bowling with surprising speed and ferocity for so early in the season. He had taken the first five wickets and the next batsman emerged from the pavilion. He was an upright military figure, with bristling white moustache and an old-fashioned I Zingari cap on his head, complete with button on the top. The sleeves of his cream shirt were buttoned down to the wrist and he had on a pair of those skeleton pads which used to be fashionable in the days of W.G. He was an imposing figure, but understandably enough he looked a trifle apprehensive at what he had to face.

The Yorkshire captain saw him coming and, realising the county were doing a bit too well, went up to Freddie and said: "This is Brigadier X. He is an important member of the county. Let him get a few." So Freddie, in his most affable and friendly manner, went up to the Brigadier as he approached the wicket and said: "Good morning, Brigadier. With my first ball I'll give you one to get off the mark." The Brigadier looked greatly relieved, but his expression changed as Freddie went on: "Aye, and with my second I'll pin thee against flippin' sightscreen!"

A CHARMING story of the great George Gunn is that when going full strength in the afternoon he threw his wicket away with the remark, " I think that I'll go and sit with the wife now and watch a little cricket."

From: ROBERTSON HARE, the actor

I ONCE took an American to watch a match at Lord's. In the first over after they arrived 15 runs were scored and at the end of the over the crowd applauded the batsman; in the next over the bowler got two wickets and once again at the end of the over the crowd applauded, obviously meaning it for the bowler. In the third over no runs were scored and to the American's mystification there was more applause from the crowd.

"Why are they applauding now?" he asked me. I replied: "Because he's just bowled a maiden over." "Oh, I see," said the American, "introducing a sex angle into the game."

From: The late BRUCE HARRIS, cricket writer

YEARS ago, when it was the custom for county cricketers to be paid match-money, out of which they paid their own fares and living expenses, it was usual to stay at the homes of the home-team players. For one match at Leicester, Albert Knight, the Leicestershire batsman, was playing host to Bill Bestwick, the Derbyshire fast bowler. Knight, who was a man of religious principles, knelt down at his bedside, revealing afterwards that he had prayed for a century on the following day. Bestwick, followed so good an example but stated afterwards that his prayer had evoked a duck for his host. Sure enough next morning Bestwick bowled Knight first ball. Knight, taking off his pads in the dressing room was asked by a friend what had happened. "Ah were ower prayed" was the simple response!

From: J. J. WARR, Middlesex and England

WHEN I was leading Middlesex against Sussex in a match at Lord's in 1960 Brian Johnston was doing the commentary during the second afternoon and started his broadcast with the words . . . "And the news here is that Warr's declared." As a result several old ladies rang up the B.B.C. anxiously enquiring what to do, and whom the war was against!

From: FRED PRICE, Middlesex and England

ON the day I made my record of seven catches in a County Championship innings, I was having a drink in the Tavern after the game, when a lady came up to me and said, "Oh, Mr. Price, I did admire your wicket-keeping today. I was so excited, I nearly fell off the balcony."

"If you had done so, madam," I replied, "on today's form I would have caught you too!"

From: PETER RICHARDSON, Kent and England

IT appears that when "Bomber" Wells was playing for Gloucestershire he was batting one day with Sam Cook. They got into a terrible tangle over a short single, with Sam just making the crease by hurling himself flat on the ground. As he lay there panting he shouted out to "Bomber": "Call!"—and "Bomber" shouted back: "Tails!"

From: JOHN ARLOTT, broadcaster—another about "Bomber"

THE Reverend David Sheppard was embroiled one day with "Bomber" Wells, and with edges past slip and short-leg was enjoying a good deal of luck.

"I should think, Vicar," said the "Bomber", "that you've been on your praying mat."

"Indeed," replied the Reverend. "But don't you pray, Brian?"

"No, I always rely on skill and a bit of luck."

"Well," said the Reverend, "which is showing the greater profit at the moment?"

THE scene: The Players' dressing-room at Lord's where Freddie Trueman was Captain of the Players against the Gentlemen. I entered, having been caught out by the Reverend David Sheppard. "I'm sorry, Skipper," I said, "but it was a good catch."

"That's all right, Peter," replied Captain Freddie. "When the Reverend puts his two hands together he stands a better chance than most of us."

From: GEOFFREY HOWARD, Secretary of Surrey County Cricket Club

AT Brisbane in 1954—ten minutes before the close of play—Trevor Bailey came on to bowl. England had been in the field all day in great heat. And Australia had scored 208 for 2. Bailey, as usual, put down the ball, paced out his run, and then took a trial run to check up on his action—without, of course, the ball. From the crowd a loud voice, obviously encouraged by a fair consumption of beer during the day, called out, "And that's your best *blank* ball terdye, Bylee!"

* * * * *

IN a Lancashire match a fast bowler was bowling on a bad wicket, and the opening batsman—who shall be nameless—had to face a number of terrifying deliveries. The first whizzed past his left ear—the second nearly knocked his cap off—and the third struck him an awful blow over the heart. He collapsed and lay on the ground—then after a minute or two got up and prepared to take strike again. The umpire asked him if he was ready—he replied, "Yes, but I would like the sightscreen moved."

"Certainly," said the umpire. "Where would you like it?"

The batsman replied, "About half way down the wicket between me and the bowler!"

From: FRANK WOOLLEY

IN a village match a batsman came in with only one pad. I pointed out to him that he only had one, and the chap said, "Yes, I know, but we only have five pads between us."

"But," said I, "you've got it on the wrong leg."

"Oh no," said the batsman, "I thought I would be batting at the other end!"

From: DENZIL BATCHELOR, writer and broadcaster

ARTHUR MAILEY was bowling for New South Wales in the famous match in which Victoria scored 1,107 against them. Mailey's figures were 4 for 362. He said afterwards, "I should have had an even better analysis if a bloke in a brown trilby hat sitting in the sixth row of the pavilion roof hadn't dropped two sitters!"

From: REG HAYTER

IN 1924 Andy Sandham was fielding on the boundary near the famous Hill at Sydney, Australia. Someone in the crowd shouted, "Sandy, ask your skipper to send out someone else, you are too ugly." After this had been going on for some time Sandy got fed up and told Arthur Gilligan who suggested that he send Patsy Hendren to field out there. Patsy made his way towards the Hill and when he had only got half way there a shout went up, " Send back Sandham."

From: E. W. DAWSON, Leicestershire and England

I WAS playing in one Gentlemen *v.* Players match at Lord's in which the Players made a huge score on the first day—the side including Jack Hobbs, Herbert Sutcliffe, Frank Woolley and Patsy Hendren. I had had a long and tiring day in the out-field and wasn't feeling any too pleased with life. As I made my way out of the Grace Gates I was confronted by a crowd of small boys—"May I have your autograph, please?" asked one of them. Not wanting to be recognised I said, "Sorry, I am not a player."

" C'oooorrrr," said the small boy. "Are you a Gentleman?"

* * * * *

IN one Leicestershire *v.* Nottinghamshire match H. Smith unwisely bowled some bumpers at Harold Larwood, much to the consternation of his own team, who realised what they would be in for when it was their turn to bat. However, he obstinately insisted on bowling short. When Leicestershire went in Larwood controlled himself very well against the early batsmen. It wasn't until Smith came in low in the order that Larwood really got down to business. He bowled a succession of terrifying bumpers, to one of which Smith got an edge which sent the ball first bounce into the hands of Sam Staples in the slips. Smith started to walk back to the pavilion, but Sam called out to him, "All right, it wasn't a catch."

"That's what *you* think," said Smith, "it's good enough for me," and continued his walk back to the dressing-room.

From: FRANK TYSON, Northamptonshire and England

WHEN I was a young man I once went in to bat against a team of first-class cricketers. My form was not very good. I missed the first ball, the next hit me on the pad, I snicked the third, and was clean bowled by the fourth. As I passed him the umpire said to me: "Aye lad, tha was lucky to make nought!"

From: The late JACK PRICE, statistician

IN his last full season with Yorkshire, Sir Leonard Hutton was not quite such an agile and quick fielder as he had been in his prime and with the pressure of captaining England upon his shoulders was perhaps not quite so enthusiastic and had lost some of his powers of concentration in the County matches. Playing in a match against Warwickshire with Fred Gardner and Norman Horner, Hutton was fielding at short square-leg close to the umpire. Gardner turned one square on the leg-side and Hutton moved slowly after it while the batsmen changed ends unseen. On picking up the ball and turning round he was amazed to find Horner at the batting end, and he was even more amazed when the late Charlie Harris, who was umpiring at square-leg, whispered in his ear: "They took 3 Len"!

* * * * *

JACK KELLY of Derbyshire, batting in the annual Bank Holiday match against Warwickshire at Edgbaston, had been stuck on 37 for a very, very long time. The crowd were snoozing in the sunshine as somnolent as the cricket and all was still and quiet except for the cries of the newspaper boys selling the evening papers. Suddenly, from one of the stands, came an anguished shout from a man waving an evening paper aloft: "Blimey, Kelly, get on with it . . . they've got you as 37 in the newspapers."

From: RONNIE WALDMAN, B.B.C.

THE Nottinghamshire Club and Ground used to play an annual match against a local village club, and the club's Captain, feeling very sure of his side's strength, warned the Nottinghamshire Secretary that he had better send a strong team down this year, otherwise they were " in for trouble." He got what he asked for, and Harold Larwood was a member of the strong side that came from Trent Bridge. The village club batted first, and their opener was a huge massive " village blacksmith " who took guard and settled down to face the great Larwood. The first ball was a typical thunderbolt. It shaved the off-stump and landed viciously in the gloves of the wicket-keeper standing very well back.

As the ball looped its way back from wicket-keeper to bowler, via slip, cover and mid-off, it was noticed that the massive batsman had not moved a muscle. His brawny arms still held the bat firmly in the block-hole, his menacing crouch was unchanged and his eyes were still fixed firmly on the far end of the wicket. A second Larwood thunderbolt—again whistling past the off-stump, had the same effect—not a move, not even a flicker of an eyelid from the vast and massive batsman. As the third ball was delivered the umpire's arm was flung out and his shriek of " No ball " echoed round the ground. For the first time the batsman unbent. He strained ponderously upwards, turned to first slip and confided, " 'E couldn't fool me, I knew 'e never 'ad one all the toime " !

From: BRIAN STATHAM, Lancashire and England

A BATSMAN batting in a very important match saw a funeral passing the ground and held up his hand to stop the bowler from bowling. He then removed his cap and stood with bowed head in silence until the funeral had passed. He then replaced his cap and continued batting, hitting the next ball for six clean out of the ground. At the end of the over the wicket-keeper said to him, " That was a very nice gesture of yours, paying such respect to the funeral procession."

" Well," said the batsman, " I've been married to her for 30 years—it was the least I could do."

From: FREDDIE TRUEMAN, Yorkshire and England

ONE day Emmott Robinson arrived at Old Trafford for the Roses Match. He was first there. He looked in the Lancashire dressing room. No-one there. He looked back into the Yorkshire dressing room. There was still no-one there so he shut the door—locked it—and, taking off his trilby, knelt down and prayed as follows:—

"Oh Lord above, thou art the greatest judge of this game of cricket which is to take place today between those two great Counties, Yorkshire and Lancashire. If Yorkshire are the best side they will win. If Lancashire are the best side they will win. If the two sides are equal or if it rains it will be a draw. But if tha will just keep out of it for three days, we will knock Hell out of 'em."

From: PETER WEST

WHEN Harold Larwood played against Wilfred Rhodes for the first time he noticed that the Yorkshire batsman when taking his stance had the front of his left foot cocked off the ground. "What's he doing that for?" said Lol to umpire Bill Reeves.

"Oh, he always stands like that," said Bill.

"He won't to me," said Larwood, and rushing up to the wicket bowled a full toss which landed with a mighty crack on Rhodes' toes. "How's that?" yelled Larwood.

"B——y painful I should think," said Reeves.

From: GORDON ROSS, Editor of "Playfair Cricket Monthly"

LEICESTERSHIRE were playing Nottinghamshire and Harold Larwood was bowling at his fastest and was in his most frightening mood. The light was very bad and he had taken four quick wickets when it was Alex Skelding's turn to bat. He came down the pavilion steps very slowly, then groped his way along the railings in front of the pavilion, shouting to the members, " Can anyone tell me where this match is being played . . . ?"

*　　*　　*　　*　　*

A SIMILAR story is told about Jack Newman when he came out to bat with Lord Tennyson, and his Lordship called down the wicket to Newman, " Why don't you appeal against the light, Jack? They won't listen to me."

To which Newman replied, " I can hear you, my Lord, but I can't see you . . . . where are you ?"

From: TOM GRAVENEY, Worcestershire and England

W. G. GRACE had just packed his bag one morning and was ready to go off and play for Gloucestershire, when a lady rushed up to his door, and when he opened it said, "Can you come quickly, Doctor, I think both my twins have got the measles."

"I am sorry, ma'am," replied the Doctor, "but I am just going off to play cricket, and can't stop. Contact me at the ground if their temperatures reach 210 for 2!"

From: MAX BYGRAVES, the famous entertainer

Wife: "Why do you play cricket so much?"
Cricketer: "It keeps me fit."
Wife: "What for?"
Cricketer: "More cricket."

*　　*　　*　　*　　*

Cricket Captain to group of children outside changing room: "Madam, you must take your children away from here; it is no place for them."
Mother: "Don't worry, they can't learn anything new; their father was a Sergeant-Major."

*　　*　　*　　*　　*

Wife at the beginning of second innings : "Let's go, John, this is where we came in."

*　　*　　*　　*　　*

An irate enthusiast, who had watched his favourite cricket team beaten, spoke to the umpire after the match: "Where's your dog?" "Dog," said the umpire, "I have no dog." "Well," said the man, "you're the first blind man I've seen without one!"

From: ALEX BANNISTER, cricket writer

WHEN Sir Donald Bradman was over here writing about the 1956 Australian tour Alex Bannister gave him a lift from London to Northampton where the Australians were playing. The route he took passed the lower reaches of Whipsnade Zoo where the animals run around in open fields. After they had passed these Alex Bannister noticed Sir Donald looking worried and rubbing his eyes, so he asked him what was the matter. "Oh," Sir Donald replied, "I really must have my eyes tested; I could have sworn I saw some kangaroos in the field we passed just now."

From: BRIAN JOHNSTON

WHEN cricketers meet they inevitably swop cricket stores, and I heard this apocryphal one last summer.

The Church of England received a challenge to a cricket match at Lord's from the Roman Catholics. The Archbishop of Canterbury was naturally keen to know what sort of chance his side would have before he took up the challenge, so he conferred with the Rev. David Sheppard, who only recommended acceptance if the C. of E. could obtain the services of Ken Barrington. The Archbishop took his advice. He summoned Barrington, specially ordained him and immediately accepted the challenge.

At half-past one on the day of the match he rang up Lord's to ask David Sheppard the score.

"What's our score?"

"I'm sorry, your Grace, but we are 44 for 9."

"How dreadful! What happened to the Rev. Kenneth Barrington?"

"Out first ball, I'm afraid."

"Who is doing all the damage then?"

"A fellow they've got called Father Trueman!!"

From: AIDAN CRAWLEY, M.P., Kent

WHEN coach at Harrow, Wilfred Rhodes was very insistent that his young charges should play all their strokes academically. One day one young 15-year-old, ignoring his mentor's instructions, thrust out his left foot, and took a mighty swing at the ball which went sailing through the air for a 100 yards or more. "That's no good," said Wilfred, "look where thar feet are." "Yes," said the boy, "but look where the ball is!"

From: ARTHUR GILLIGAN, Sussex and England

ONCE when broadcasting one of the Test Matches from Australia, a message was sent to me that a lady wished to speak to me outside the pavilion. I went down and the lady said, " Will you give this packet to Mr. Statham?"

" What is it ?" I asked.

" It's a packet of bicarbonate of soda," was her reply.

" What on earth does Mr. Statham want with that?"

" Oh," she said, " I have just heard you say on the air that Brian Statham was bowling with the wind !"

From: JOHN WOODCOCK, cricket writer

DURING the M.C.C. tour at a reception in Perth, Freddie Trueman was talking to the Rev. D.S. when the Bishop of Perth passed by, resplendent in his gaiters and his pectoral cross. Freddie saw him and out of the corner of his mouth said to David Sheppard: "Is that your senior pro?"

From: BILL BOWES, Yorkshire and England

I RETURNED to my home near Leeds one Saturday evening when a Test Match at Old Trafford had been abandoned because of heavy rain. On getting out of the train I was somewhat embarrassed to read on a newspaper placard—"OLD TRAFFORD SWAMPED BY BILL BOWES."

From: LOUIS DUFFUS, South African cricket writer

DURING the South African tour of Australia in 1931-32, Don Bradman had a most enjoyable time and thrashed the Springbok bowlers to all quarters of the field every time he met them.

Towards the end of the tour A. J. "Sandy" Bell was in a newspaper office when Bradman looked in for a moment. After a few words Bradman walked out of the room and Bell said in wonder, "So *that's* what his back looks like; it's the first time I have seen it this tour."

From: REX ALSTON, radio commentator

I WAS once doing a commentary at Lord's with E. W. Swanton as my summariser, to whom I referred for comment between the overs. The last ball of one over which I was describing got the edge of a batsman's bat and just dropped short of first slip who made a great effort to catch it. With my eyes still on the wicket I said: "Well, that was a very near thing for the batsman; though I don't really think we can call it a chance. However, it's the end of the over so let's ask Jim Swanton what he thought." I turned round and, to my horror, found an empty seat beside me with the following notice written on a piece of paper—"Have gone to spend a penny. Back in a minute. Jim."

From: MICHAEL MELFORD, cricket writer

THE first day of Alec Skelding's benefit match was played in terrible weather, it was very cold and there was no crowd; just a lonely dog watching the play. Telling somebody about the match in later years he said: "Play took place before a keen wind."

From: SIR ALEC DOUGLAS-HOME, M.P., Middlesex

THIS happened to an Eton contemporary in a school match when he was trying to get into the XI.

He was hit by the ball plumb in the middle of his pads with both legs right in front of his wicket and there was a unanimous appeal from his opponents.

"Not out," said the school umpire.

When, later, he reached the umpire's end the boy said: "I must have been jolly nearly out that time!"

"My boy," said the umpire, "you was so jolly nearly out that if you had been one of the visiting side you would have been!"

Two from: PETER RICHARDSON

ROLY JENKINS, when asked what he thought of the efficiency of modern day cricket legislators, replied :

"Most County Cricket Committee men are so ignorant of the game as it is played today that they think an in-swinger is part of the brass section in Ted Heath's band."

*   *   *   *   *

WORCESTERSHIRE were playing Scotland and Roly Jenkins was bowling to the Rev. J. Aitchison, the home side's best batsman. He kept playing and missing at Roly's leg breaks and googlies, and was also lucky euough to get away with a couple of l.b.w. decisions which we thought were out. After about a quarter of an hour of this, Roly was getting a bit annoyed. Until at last the Rev. was given out to a decision which he thought himself unlucky to get. "Unlucky!" said Roly. "If I'd have had as much luck as him my name wouldn't be the Rev. Aitchison—it would be the Archbishop of Canterbury!"

From: The REV. EMRYS WALTERS, Member of Sussex Cricket Committee

IN a match between two teams of clergy the local Bishop opened the innings. A young Curate was the opening bowler, and in due deference to the Bishop's office sent up a slow half-volley with the intention of helping the portly Bishop to " get off the mark." The Bishop smote the ball straight out of the ground and turned to the young Curate saying, " I am sorry, young man, but I seem to have hit you out of your Parish." The Curate grinned sheepishly, and feeling rather peeved walked slowly back to his mark. He turned, ran in, and sent down a vicious bumper. This hit the Bishop in the midriff and he collapsed to the ground in agony. The young Curate rushed up and said, "I am sorry, M'Lord, but I seem to have hit you in the middle of your Diocese."

From: DUDLEY NOURSE (Jnr.), Past Captain of South Africa

WHEN England met South Africa in the First Test at Birmingham in 1924, H. W. Taylor won the toss and sent England in to bat. They stayed at the wicket the whole of the Saturday. The Manager of the tourists had other business to attend to on Monday morning and did not arrive at the ground until lunch-time. When he saw the scoreboard reading 29 for no wicket he chided his players saying, " You've been a bit slow this morning, haven't you ? This is not the sort of stuff to bring the crowds in." When told that this was South Africa's second innings, it took some little while before he could be convinced that he was not having his leg pulled . . . .

From: BRIAN JOHNSTON

A T an Edgbaston Test during one of my spells off from the microphone I sat next to Cyril Walters, surely one of the most graceful batsmen ever to play for England. During a lull in the play he told me a story about a friend of his who was driving his brand-new Bentley down a very narrow country lane. An elderly lady in an old Austin came towards him and by stopping and going right into the ditch on his left he was just able to make room for the old lady to steer slowly past him. As she went by she stuck her head out of the window and shouted "Pig!" Somewhat taken aback he yelled back, "You silly old faggot!" and feeling highly incensed drove on round the next corner, where he came on a pig standing in the middle of the road!

From: MAURICE LEYLAND, Yorkshire and England

I N the Roses Match at Headingley in 1924 Yorkshire wanted only 58 runs to win in the second innings and were bowled out for 33. A supporter walking past the local asylum on his way home was asked for the result of the match by an inmate, who on being told, said, "Blimey they'll go crackers in here when I tell 'em that!"

From: PETER MAY, Surrey and England

ONE day Surrey were playing an away match at a seaside resort, and during one of the intervals Alec Bedser was followed by a long line of children eager to get his autograph when he got to the steps of the pavilion. The good-natured bowler turned round and said to them, "Who do you think I am, the Pied Piper of Hambledon?"

From: PETER CRANMER, Warwickshire

WARWICKSHIRE were batting against Derbyshire in the late 'forties. They collapsed against some fine bowling by Cliff Gladwin, and as each batsman returned to the Warwickshire dressing-room he had a different excuse to give. "That one swung in and knocked out my leg stump"—"Mine pitched on the leg stump and took the off bail"—"He bowled me with a slow swinging yorker"—and so on. Eric Hollies was sitting quietly in a corner apparently asleep. But each time a batsman described the sort of ball with which Gladwin had bowled him Eric wrote something down on a piece of paper. When it came to his turn to bat at No. 11 as usual he walked out holding his bat in one hand and the piece of paper in the other. As he passed Gladwin on his way up the pitch, he handed him the paper and said: "Bowl them in that order, Cliff, and I'll be all right."

From: BRIAN JOHNSTON

DURING the Oval Test, Lord Cobham was telling me about one of his shortest and certainly luckiest innings in first-class cricket. As Charles Lyttelton he was playing for Worcestershire against Gloucestershire in the 'thirties. When he went in to bat Charlie Parker was bowling. Off his first ball he was missed at slip by Wally Hammond of all people—a chance to his right hand. The next ball hit the stumps without removing the bails. The third, believe it or not, went to Hammond's *left* hand and was dropped. The fourth ball bowled him. As he made his way back, somewhat embarrassed, to the pavilion he passed Charlie Barnett who was fielding at third man. "Bad luck, skipper," he said. "You were never quite in!"

From: LES AMES, Kent and England

A WELL-KNOWN Test cricketer was offered 100 guineas
for a brief appearance on I.T.V. to advertise a certain
brand of cigarettes. For some reason or other he could
not appear, and suggested another Test player. This also
proved fruitless and eventually the advertising agents found
an old village cricketer aged 80, who had smoked 50 of those
cigarettes a day for the last 60 years. They explained to him
that although his appearance on TV would be only 1 minute,
the film and rehearsal would take at least an hour, and so
they wanted him at the studio at 10.0 a.m. the following
morning. "Oh, blow that," he said, "I can't manage it as
early as that—I don't finish coughing until midday."

From: D. V. P. WRIGHT, Kent and England

JUST before the War Kent were playing Yorkshire at
Bradford, at a time when Hedley Verity was contributing
what he called his "Diary" to a local newspaper. In
this diary he put all the high scores, wickets and brilliant
pieces of fielding. Kent were batting with Les Ames at one
end and me at the other, and Les received an off-spinner
which was a little short of a length from George Macaulay.
The ball did not turn very much, and Les was able to cut it
pretty hard. Verity was standing in the gully, and the ball
came swiftly to him, hitting him hard on the wrist. Hedley
clutched at the ball but fell backwards and it dropped to the
ground. As quick as lightning George Macaulay shouted up
the wicket: "Now then, put that in the b . . . Diary."

From: HERBERT SUTCLIFFE, Yorkshire and England

ON January 1st, 1925, Hobbs and I batted all day against Australia in Melbourne, putting on 283 for the opening partnership, in reply to what was then a record Test total of 600 runs by Australia. There were 75,000 people on the ground, and as the day wore on they began to barrack their team more and more. (It is worth remembering perhaps that the bowlers included Jack Gregory, Charlie Kelleway, Arthur Mailey and Arthur Richardson.) But the barrackers were merciless on them, " You'll never get 'em out—you'll have to burn 'em out—send for the Fire Brigade, they'll get 'em out—put the roller on—put the clock on— etc., etc." But the culminating point of the whole day's batting came between the tea interval and the close of play. There was a momentary silence which was broken by a terrific raucous voice which yelled out, "Send for Nurse Blank, she'll get the b . . . . s out !"

(Nurse Blank was a well-known midwife who shortly before the Test Match had made the headlines in an abortion case!)

From: ALF GOVER, Surrey and England

AS a young 19 year old, I arrived at Lord's for my first Middlesex *v.* Surrey match. When I got to the old "Pro's" dressing room, only one other person was there—the great Patsy Hendren. "Hello, young chap," he called out, "what's your name?"

"Alf Gover, Sir."

"What do you do?"

"I bowl."

"Quick?" said Patsy.

"Very quick," I answered proudly. Patsy looked round the room to make sure that he was not overheard, came over to me and said, very confidentially: "Look, son, I don't mind quick bowling, you can push it down at me as fast as you like, only—" another conspiratorial glance round—"only I don't like 'em if they are pitched short. You know this is my home ground and they like me to get a few. My peepers aren't as good as they were and I can't pick up the ball as fast as I used to, so keep them well up to me, won't you?" I pondered on this self-admitted fear of the great England and Middlesex batsman and decided that there was a great chance for me to make my name.

I happened to be bowling from the Pavilion end when he came in, and said to myself: "Ah, here's that old man who can't see and doesn't like short-pitched balls—so here goes." My first ball to him was very short, just outside the leg stump and as fast as I could bowl it. It was promptly hooked for six into the Tavern. "Fluke," I said to myself and sent him down a similar short ball, only this time on the middle stump. Patsy took two steps back and cut it for four past third man. "I've got him scared now—he's running away," I said to myself as I walked back to my mark. Down came my third ball just the same as the other two and it went sailing away for six into the Mound Stand.

At the end of the over Jack Hobbs came across to me from cover. "What are you bowling short at Mr. Hendren for, son?"

"He's afraid of them," I answered.

The "Master" looked at me in amazement. "Who told you that?" he asked.

"He did, Mr. Hobbs," I said.

"Dont be silly," he replied. "Don't you know he's the best hooker of fast bowling in the world. And what's more, young man, I'd remind you he's an Irishman and every night he kisses the Blarney Stone!"

And so I learnt to my cost—and Surrey's—that not only was Patsy Hendren one of England's greatest batsmen and one of the best hookers the world has ever known, but also its most superb leg-puller.

* * * * *

From: ARTHUR PHEBEY, Kent

A CRICKETER who was asked what he was going to do during the winter months—and wanting to be in the current fashion—said, " Oh, I shall write a book of course."

" Oh," said the questioner, " what on ? "

The cricketer being fairly learned said, " On Ethics."

" Oh," said his friend, " I thought you played for Sussex."

From: BUD FLANAGAN, of the Crazy Gang

IT was a Sunday in Australia, and Percy Chapman and Patsy Hendren decided to get away from it all and borrowed a car for a run into the country. After a few miles they went round a corner and saw a cricket match about to start in a field adjoining the road. As all cricketers are wont to do—they stopped the car with the intention of watching the game for a few minutes. The car no sooner stopped than an Australian strolled over to the car and said, " Do either of you chaps play cricket?"

Chapman pointed to Patsy and said, " He plays a little."

" Good Oh," said the fellow, " we are a man short ; will you make up for us ?"

Although it was Patsy's day off he obliged, and as his adopted side were fielding the captain sent him out to long-on. Patsy went to the allotted position, and as the field was on a slope he was out of sight of the pitch. He had nothing to do except throw the ball in occasionally. He was lost to sight for a long time when at last a towering hit was sent in his direction. Patsy caught the ball and ran up the hill shouting, "I caught it, I caught it." The batsman looked at him with daggers drawn—it was *his* captain. "You lunatic—*they* were out twenty minutes ago. *We* are batting now!"

From: BRIAN STATHAM, Lancashire and England

KEN GRIEVES boasts to be the first cricketer to "bag a pair" in front of eight million spectators. He got two 0's and on each occasion when he was dismissed, the Television commentary was in progress. His small daughter, watching the game with her mother at home, said, " Why is Daddy going into that big house so soon ; doesn't he like playing with those other Masters ? "

Another from BRIAN STATHAM

GEORGE GUNN, when playing for Nottinghamshire against Glamorgan, started to walk off the field at at half-past one with the impression that it was time for lunch. However, under the conditions for that match, lunch was not due to be taken until 2.00 p.m. and Gunn was recalled to continue his innings ; he lifted his bat away from the next ball—was comprehensibly bowled—making no attempt to play the ball—and as he retired to the pavilion, said " You can have your lunch, gentlemen, when you like, but I always take mine at 1.30 p.m."

Another from the late ROY WEBBER

GUBBY ALLEN, Chairman of the England Test Selectors in 1956, produced a nap hand of successes. In the First Test at Nottingham he chose Peter Richardson and Colin Cowdrey to open the innings and they had a second innings partnership of 151. At Lord's he left Tony Lock out of the England team. On the morning of the match, and before the close of play, that player had gone down with suspected appendicitis. In the Third Test he brought back Cyril Washbrook from retirement and after England had lost three cheap wickets Cyril scored 98 and England won by an innings. At Manchester David Sheppard was brought back and he also scored a century. Finally, at the Oval, Denis Compton, who had only just returned after a serious knee operation, was brought into the side and he scored 94. At the end of this match someone remarked to Allen—"What are you going to try next?—Walking on water?"

From: ARTHUR ASKEY, the comedian

THE scene: Yorkshire v. Lancashire—Roses Match at Sheffield.

Father arrived early and kept a spare seat for his son —who arrived half-an-hour after the start of play, breathless and pale with excitement. "Father," he said, "I've got some terrible news for thee—house is on fire."

"Aye—"

"Mother's been taken to hospital with bad burns—"

"Aye—"

"And she says she forgot to send Insurance money—"

"Aye, and I've got bad news for thee too—'Utton's out!"

From: ROBERTSON HARE

PETER MAY giving the England Test Team a "pep" talk before going out to field, ended with the historic quotation—(in brief) "England expects!" . . . Sobers, passing by at that moment, overheard the famous words, and remarked with a smile, "No doubt that's why they call her the '*Mother* Country'!"

From: The late GEORGE DUCKWORTH, Lancashire and England

ABOUT a certain Test bowler who was known to be a chucker, Brian Statham remarked, "He ought to get the job as Professional at HURLingham!"

From: The late PAT O'SHAUGHNESSY

ON the first day at a Test Match at Edgbaston I was sitting behind a very obvious Birmingham businessman, who seemed to be following the game very keenly. I got into conversation with him and criticised and watched the game with him all day. The same thing happened on the Friday. At the close of play I said to the man: "Well, I suppose I shall be seeing you Saturday morning."

"What," said the man, "me watch cricket on my day off? Not likely!"

From: R. J. G. McCRUDDEN, Secretary of Gloucestershire

IN a match against Gloucestershire Brian Close was fielding at forward short leg with Freddie Trueman bowling. Martin Young received a short ball which he hit right in the middle of the bat. It hit Close on the right side of the head and rebounded to first slip who caught it!

Close seemed none the worse but when he returned to the pavilion at the next interval I asked him: "That was a terrible blow; aren't you worried standing so near? What *would* have happened if the ball had hit you slap between the eyes?"

"He'd have been caught at cover," replied the indomitable Yorkshire captain!

From: MAX BYGRAVES

A BATSMAN was given out l.b.w. and strongly disagreed with the umpire's decision. However, he restrained himself until the next interval when he went up to a man in a white coat and said: "Umpire, I wasn't out; you need your eyes tested." "Oh, I do, do I?" said the man. "Well you'd better have yours tested too, I'm selling ice cream!"

From: COLIN COWDREY, Kent and England

ON our first visit to Melbourne during the last tour of Australia our Manager, the Duke of Norfolk, captained a team of M.C.C. golfers against the Royal Melbourne Golf Club, who gave us a sound beating. That very morning we had all been reading the headlines in the papers which said that the M.C.C. players were playing far too much golf and were not paying enough attention to the job in hand. So you can imagine the laughter which greeted the Duke at the end of the day, when he said in an apologetic speech to our hosts: "I am sorry we didn't play better golf. We're all a bit out of practice. We have been playing too much cricket!"

From: S. C. GRIFFITH, Secretary of M.C.C. (telling the story against himself)

WHEN Secretary of Sussex I was next in to bat at a match at Hove, and was in the middle of a telephone conversation when a wicket fell. "Can you hold on for a moment," I said, "I've got to go in to bat, but I'll be back in a moment" . . . and I was!

But this is not as bad as a County Secretary a few years ago; he used to sign his letters before he went in to bat and blot them after he was out!

O N a hot and sticky day during the Oval Test Match of 1938, Bill O'Reilly bowled over after over against the bats of Len Hutton and Maurice Leyland. From time to time he asked for an l.b.w. decision, and finally at about a-quarter-to-six with England 300 for 1 he trapped one of the batsmen on the back foot plumb in front of the lot. O'Reilly reeled round with a snarl and said, "Well, how was that one, 'ump?"

" 'Ump?—you've been giving me the ruddy 'ump all day. Not out."

*   *   *   *   *

I N a village match the bowler was hit for 20 runs off the first five balls of an over. Before the delivery of the last ball the batsman was worried by a wasp buzzing round his head. He swiped at it—hit it—but didn't kill it. No-one knew quite what to do with the wounded wasp. But the wicket-keeper suggested, "Put it on the good length spot—it will be quite safe there."

I WAS reporting one of the Test Matches during the 1960 Test rubber between England and South Africa for the *Daily Express*. I was describing a confident l.b.w. appeal which had been turned down by the umpire, and wrote, "The ball would certainly have missed the off and leg stumps, but I can't say the same about the middle!"

From: The late ARTHUR WRIGLEY

A MAN, whose wife was in hospital expecting a baby, telephoned one afternoon to see what the news was. By mistake he got the local cricket ground. When he asked what was the latest position the reply came back, " There are seven out already, and the last two were ducks!"

*   *   *   *   *

D URING a village match the umpire was heckled by supporters of the home side. After a while he left the field and went and sat down in a deckchair among the noisy spectators. " What's the idea?" he was asked.
" It appears you get the best view from here," he replied.

*   *   *   *   *

T HE bowler had appealed for l.b.w. The village umpire said to the batsman, " Take your legs out of the way, I can't see the wicket."

From: TREVOR HOWARD, actor

A LEC SKELDING was umpiring a match where the bowler had a complete set of false teeth. As he delivered a particularly fast ball all his teeth dropped out. The ball hit the batsman on the pad, and the bowler turned round and mouthed unintelligible noises. Alec, quick to see what had happened, said, " I beg your pardon I cannot tell what you say." The bowler tried again but Alec still pretended he could not distinguish the words, so the bowler stooped down, recovered his dentures covered in dust, replaced them and turning round, said, " How's that?"
" Not out," said Alec.

[70]

From: NORMAN YARDLEY.

ON returning home from the Third Test Match against West Indies at Nottingham in 1950, where I had just captained England for the last time, I was greeted by my wife with the remark, "Do you know what they did to you on Television today?" When I said, "No," she went on to tell me that towards the end of the big partnership between Weekes and Worrell on Saturday, when they added a record 283 for the 4th wicket, Brian Johnston doing the television commentary said, " England are in a very bad position, I wonder what Norman Yardley is going to do about it; let's put the camera on him and have a look." Unfortunately, at this particular moment I was scratching myself in a rather embarrassing place. This horrified my wife, but she said that at least B.J. had the decency to add, "Obviously it's a very ticklish problem!"

From: DESMOND EAGAR, ex-Captain and now Secretary of Hampshire

THE other day I was told a delightful story about that great Hampshire character George Brown. He had been put on to bowl by Lord Tennyson and bowled the first ball in a large sweater. "Take your sweater off, George," said Tennyson. George did so, and underneath was another thick sweater. He bowled again and immediately his lordship ordered him to remove this second sweater. George took it off and to the surprise of everyone revealed a waistcoat with an enormous watch and chain!

From: ARTHUR ASKEY, the comedian.

AS you know I am mad keen on cricket and during the last visit of the Australians to England, having been watching the television at home, I went out of the room for a moment.

My daughter Anthea, who was also watching, called out: "Come quick, daddy, one of the commentators is talking about you." I rushed into the room and asked what the commentator had said. "Well, I think it must have been about you," she said, "he was talking about someone having two silly short legs."

From: BRIAN JOHNSTON

A County cricketer was playing in a Sunday Benefit Match on a very hot and sultry day in June. When the time came for lunch he partook of his refreshments—both solid and liquid—in generous measure. Shortly after the interval two or three wickets fell quickly and the batsman, on going out from the pavilion, said to his Captain, "What shall I do? I shall see three balls."

"That's all right," said his Skipper, "hit the middle one." The batsman staggered to the wicket with a slightly wavy gait—took guard—hit wildly at the first ball he received and saw his middle stump knocked out of the ground. On returning to the pavilion his Captain said to him, "What was the matter with you? Why didn't you hit the middle ball as I told you to?"

"I did," said the batsman, "but you didn't tell me which bat to use."

From: ARTHUR WOOD, Yorkshire and England

YORKSHIRE were playing the South Africans at Sheffield, and the late H. B. Cameron went in to face the bowling of Hedley Verity. Cameron took guard and hit the first ball over the pavilion for six. The next three balls all went for four and the last two for six each, making 30 runs off the over. When Verity passed me at the end of the over,

his face was as long as a collie's, but I said, "You don't want to worry, Hedley, you've got him in two minds."

"Two minds?" said Verity. "What do you mean, two minds?"

"Oh," said I, "he doesn't know whether to hit you for four or six."

From: MAURICE ALLOM, Surrey and England

DURING the Surrey and Yorkshire match at the Oval in 1929, I went away to the seaside on the Saturday night, and whilst bathing in the swimming pool on the Sunday night I trod on a bottle. I cut my instep very badly, resulting in three or four stitches and my being out of action for the rest of the season. The *Evening Standard* reported the incident the following day, but the Sub-Editor got things slightly muddled, and reported it as follows: "M. J. C. Allom was unable to take any further part in the match between Surrey and Yorkshire because he cut his foot on a broken bottle while batting at the Oval yesterday."

From: FRANK LEE, Middlesex and Somerset

IN 1929 when making my first appearance against Nottinghamshire, I went in to bat in the second innings with the prospect of obtaining the cricketer's dreaded pair. I had landed a nought in the first innings facing the great Harold Larwood, and watching Harold's run up to bowl from 22 yards distance was, I felt, similar to the feelings of a rabbit with a stoat approaching. As I commenced my bat uplift something hit it, that something proving to be the ball which flew off the edge between the many slips and gullys and went rapidly to the third-man fieldsman. Breathing thankfully I ran to the other end where Jim Street, the umpire, was standing. He turned to me and whispered: "A nice **lad**, Harold, he bowled you a slow one."

From: PETER MAY.

IN 1957 in one of the Test Matches against the West Indies they were batting when rain stopped play—obviously an answer to a Captain's prayer with such bowlers as Tony Lock and Jim Laker in his side. When the rain stopped Goddard and I went out to inspect the wicket, and Goddard ruefully considered the prospect of batting against two such fine spinners on a rain-affected wicket. He had been *praying* that the rain would continue and said to me, "You know this is hardly fair on us, you have a professional in your side." I glanced at the pavilion and there on the balcony was the Reverend David Sheppard. I then understood what was behind Goddard's remark.

From: KEN BARRINGTON, Surrey and England

THE Hillites had plenty of cause for barracking in this Fifth Test. On the first morning, when England scored only 16 in the first hour, a hoarse voice shouted out, "Send for Trevor Bailey. He'd liven things up!"

On the last day, when Lawry took four hours to make 45, he did hit a couple of 4's in succession off two loose balls from Tom Graveney, but soon relapsed into his defensive role. This was too much for one barracker who shouted, "Come on, Lightning, strike again."

From: JOHN SNAGGE, B.B.C.

ANNOUNCER on radio reading cricket scores . . . Yorkshire 232 all out, Hutton ill—I'm sorry, Hutton one hundred and eleven."

From: MR. F. D. BILLHAM, a keen follower of cricket.

THE game: Middlesex *v.* Hampshire at Lord's. The umpire: "Bill" Reeves, former Essex player. Middlesex batting, with H. J. Enthoven the non-striker, and Jack Newman bowling for Hampshire. The striker played the ball towards mid-on and called for a run; but the bowler, running across to the ball, inadvertently impeded Enthoven, who fell and was out of his ground when the bowler's wicket was broken. Reeves, however, gave him not out, on the grounds that he had been baulked by the bowler. Tennyson, the Hampshire captain, reported the matter and, after a week, Reeves was called before the M.C.C. Committee. Lord Hawke, in the chair, called upon Reeves to describe the incident in his own words. Having done so, he waited nervously for the Committee's decision; but after what seemed to be an interminable interval, he could no longer contain himself and burst out: "Well, my lord, what would you have done if you had been the umpire?" Lord Hawke, taken aback, replied: "Well, I don't know. I don't know." Then Reeves: "A damned fine umpire you'd make, my lord. You've had a week to think about it; I only had a second!" The story went that Lord Hawke burst out laughing and that Reeves got away with a caution.

From: R. E. S. WYATT, Warwickshire, Worcestershire and England

ONE day Sutcliffe and I had put on 140 for the first wicket in a Test Match at Sydney. A gentleman on the Hill who had apparently come to watch Wally Hammond bat, shouted at the top of his voice, "Come on, Wyatt, get out. We've seen all your strokes, and you've got them all but one, and it will be a damn good job when you've got that one—it's sunstroke!"

From: ANDREW SANDHAM, Surrey

SURREY were playing Middlesex at the Oval and Bill Reeves was one of the umpires. Nigel Haig opened the bowling and as usual I went in first for Surrey. As you know I am not very tall and a ball from Haig hit me in the navel and there was a loud appeal. "Not out," said Reeves. "Why not?" asked Haig. "Too high," said Reeves. Haig went back to his mark muttering, possibly thinking that even if a ball hit a little chap like me on the head it couldn't be too high. A few balls later a beautiful ball beat me all ends up and hit me on the pads. "What about that one then?" yelled Haig. "Not out," said Reeves. "Why not?" said Haig. "Too low!" said Reeves—and that ended all arguments for that day!

From: NEVILLE CARDUS

DICK TYLDESLEY played for England in the Leeds Test of 1930 when Sir Donald Bradman made 309 not out on the first day. Dick had been toiling away all day with his leg breaks (he finally finished with 2 for 104). So that evening I thought he deserved a drink, and over a pint said to him, "This Bradman—he's pretty good, isn't he?" Dick replied: "I don't know about that. But he's no good to me."

From: H.H. MAHARAJA GAEKWAR OF BARODA

WHEN we visited Sheffield during the Indian tour which I managed in 1959 I met a Yorkshire friend of mine who is mad keen on cricket but who has a wooden left leg. He used to play a lot in spite of it and some years ago before the war was asked to play for a scratch side against a team at Ampleforth. When his side won the toss he went in first and after taking guard looked up to see who the bowler was, but could only see a distant figure by the sightscreen. He turned round to ask the wicket-keeper but found the latter was standing yards back, very nearly by the sightscreen at the other end. Finally he asked one of the battery of short legs for the bowler's name. "Oh, it's the fast bowler the Rev. P. R. Utley, who is a master here. You know, the chap who took all those Yorkshire wickets for Hampshire last week." My friend quailed and decided the best thing was to keep bat and pad very close together and not to lift the bat from the block hole. He never saw the first ball which hit the back of his wooden leg with an enormous crack and went flying off to the long leg boundary. To his surprise he saw the umpire signal four runs. The same thing happened to the next ball. A sound of splintering wood and another hit for four signalled. The third ball, alas, was straighter and knocked his off-stump out of the ground. But at least he had hit two fours off a first-class fast bowler, and with no damage done which a carpenter couldn't put right.

From: RICHIE BENAUD, Australia

ON the Sunday of the Edgbaston Test Match in 1965 Brian Johnston and I were asked by John Woodcock to play for a team of masters from the Dragon School at Oxford in their annual match against a boys' club from Notting Hill. We had a most enjoyable game and I was bowling when the last man came in. Brian as usual was behind "the timbers", and the batsman went down the pitch to one of my leg breaks, missed it and was stumped by Brian, who was very pleased about this and told me it proved that he had lost none of his old skill and quickness with the gloves. However, a few minutes later he was somewhat staggered when the Bursar, who had been fielding, came up to him and said, "Well stumped. And I would also like to congratulate you on the sporting way you tried to give him time to get back!"

From: GARFIELD SOBERS, West Indies

IN a Central Lancashire League match a batsman snicked the ball hard on to his pads, from where it went down towards long leg. He ran one run, but was amazed on approaching the other end, to hear the bowler appealing for l.b.w. To his horror the umpire then put his finger up. Unable to contain himself the batsman blurted out, "I can't be out l.b.w. I hit it." "I know you did," said the umpire. "I'm only signalling byes."

From: DONALD CARR, Assistant Secretary of M.C.C.

A RECENTLY arrived diplomat from one of the Iron Curtain countries was looking for a flat in London, preferably in St. John's Wood. Before he left his country he had been briefed about various British customs and institutions. It had been impressed on him that a queer game called cricket was a religion with most people in England. Accordingly he rang up an estate agent in St. John's Wood and said he wanted a flat—"if possible somewhere near your Jesus Cricket Ground."

EST. 1788

From: Sir Donald Bradman, Australia

SURPRISINGLY enough my favourite story comes from a match which otherwise does not hold very pleasant memories for me—the Fifth Test at the Oval in 1938. Arthur Wood, the Yorkshire wicket-keeper, who had been called in to play at the last moment went in to bat at No. 8 when the score was 770 for 6. When he returned to the pavilion after a hard-hit 53, he and Joe Hardstaff had put on another 106 runs and the score stood at 876 for 7. As Arthur made his way back up the pavilion steps, he turned to a member and said, "Just like me to get out in a crisis."

From: Graham McKenzie, Australia

DURING the M.C.C. tour of Australia in 1965–66 Bill Lawry made a succession of large scores in the Tests, but always took a mighty long time about it. On one occasion an Australian barracker could stand it no longer. "What's the matter, Lawry?" he shouted, "being so careful. Have you taken the Pill?"

From: David Frost of "That Was the Week That Was" and "Not So Much a Programme . . ."

I WAS playing in a charity match one Sunday and was lucky enough to share in quite a big partnership with Everton Weekes. When the latter was finally out the commentator on the public address aptly remarked, "That was the Weekes—that was!"

From: Bert Sutcliffe, New Zealand

ON my last trip to England Valerie Warr told of an amusing thing which happened to her when her husband John was captain of Middlesex. The latter were playing away against Glamorgan at Neath during Ascot week so she had to go to the races alone. A rather posh gentleman asked her where her husband was. "Oh, he's playing cricket at Neath," she replied. "Really," said the p.g. "I had no idea they played cricket in the South of France!"

From: NEIL HAWKE, Australia

THE scene was an attractive little cricket ground set in picturesque Adelaide Hills in sunny South Australia.

The cricket standard was of dubious quality, but Australia's reserve wicket-keeper, Barry Jarman, stared at a new arrival at the batting crease. It was none other than ace Aussie jockey Bill Pyers, now busily riding winners in France. The observant Jarman at once noticed an expensive watch on Pyers' wrist and said immediately, "Hey, Billy, did you know you still have your watch on?" As quick as a flash the bright-witted Pyers looked at it and replied, "It's okay, I use it to time my shots."

From: JOHN REID, New Zealand

WHEN I was last in England I heard a good but perhaps unlikely story about that cheerful character, Dave Sydenham, who was a chiropodist, when he was not playing cricket for Surrey. The story goes that during the winter he was driving along in his car and was waved down by a man standing by a car at the roadside. "Thanks for stopping," said the man, "I'm afraid I have broken down. Are you an engineer by any chance?" "No," said Sydenham, "I'm a chiropodist." "Fine," said the man, "then in that case you can give me a tow!"

From: ROY MCLEAN, South Africa

THIS is a story about the customary annual council match, between Durban and Pietermaritzburg. The mayor and skipper of Durban had represented his side for 15 years, and during that period had only captured 2 wickets and made 17 runs, but never had he held a catch. The game was duly played in Durban and after a few wickets fell, in strode the mayor of Pietermaritzburg to take strike. All of a sudden, he took an almighty swing and the ball went soaring into the heavens straight to the Durban skipper. His apprehension was terrific and in the dying moments he closed his eyes and the ball landed safely in his left hand. His jubilation was fantastic —tossing the ball in the air and then lying down and rolling the ball on his forehead—his first catch ever in such class cricket. He then held the ball aloft to receive the congratulations of his team mates, but he was confronted by a rather irate mid-on who said, "For God's sake throw the ball back—it was a NO-BALL and the batsmen have run 7 already!"

From: JOHN WAITE, South Africa

DURING the last New Zealand tour to South Africa John Reid enjoyed his best ever season and batted quite magnificently and with remarkable consistency.

Playing for the South African Colts XI against these Tourists at East London, Tiger Lance, this time in the role of bowler, was suffering rather a cruel hammering from the bat of John Reid who had amassed yet another superb century. "What do I do now?" asked Tiger to his mid-off as he walked back to his bowling mark. "Oh, I don't know—just pray to God," was mid-off's reply. "I can't,' said Tiger, 'he's batting!"

From: CHARLES FORTUNE, South African broadcaster

FROM time to time over 20 years I have been allowed to broadcast cricket and for 20 years my friends have declared that too little by way of scores and too much by way of birds, beasts and flowers creep into the commentary. But one day, not so long ago, consolation for these outrageous slings and arrows came along. She was middle aged, floated rather than walked. As she came across the room she said: "Oh, Mr. Fortune, I so wanted to meet you. I listen for hours to the cricket and I absolutely adore your little ANTIDOTES."

From: GRAEME POLLOCK, South Africa

ONE of the best stories I've heard was one told me during the Trent Bridge Test Match in 1965. It was about the late Charlie Harris of Nottinghamshire whom, of course, I never knew but who was evidently a pretty remarkable character. Fielding in the deep, Charlie dislocated his shoulder when throwing the ball to the wicket-keeper. He was taken off to hospital and into the operating theatre, where—without an anaesthetic—the surgeon tried to put it back. This was a very painful process, and Charlie Harris was not very quiet during the manipulation. Eventually the operating room sister said: "Mr. Harris, there is a woman in the next room who is having a baby, and she is not making half the fuss that you are." "No," said Charlie, "but I bet she would be if they were trying to put it back!"

From: HANIF MOHAMMED, Pakistan

IN 1958 at Bridgetown against the West Indies, I played my marathon innings of 337 which lasted for 16 hours 13 minutes. Shortly afterwards I was told an amusing story about this innings, but whether it is true or not I cannot promise. Evidently a West Indian supporter, perched perilously on a branch of a tree, stuck it for most of the day but then falling asleep either from the heat or boredom (!) fell with a resounding crash to the ground and knocked himself out. He was taken off to hospital where he was unconscious for some time. When he eventually came round one of the hospital nurses told him he'd been "out" for two hours. Quick as a flash he exclaimed: "I only hope Hanif has been too"

From: COLIN COWDREY, Kent and England

DURING Peter May's tour of Australia in 1958–59 M.C.C. suffered so many injuries that they had to send back for reinforcements. Ted Dexter and John Mortimore were flown out to join us. Two elderly members of a well-known club in St. James's Street were discussing the situation. One of them said to the other: "I see that M.C.C. have had so many injuries that they're sending out some more players." "Yes," said the other, "I've just read that they're sending Mortimore." "How many?" exclaimed the first member. "*Forty* more! I didn't know it was as bad as that!"

From: BRIAN BOOTH, Australia

DURING the Australian cricket tour of England 1964, the Australians were playing Nottingham at Trent Bridge. Notts were batting in their first innings and were 9 wickets down for 97 (I think) when in came "Bomber" Wells at number 11. We had been told that he was a great personality so expected something amusing from him. We knew him as a good off spinner, but as a batsman, one who had taken more wickets than runs. When he arrived at the crease, the umpire said to "Bomber", "What would you like?" (meaning what guard). "Bomber" looked round the field and longingly at the score-board—muttered, "9 for 97—about the only thing you can give me, ump, is Help!"

From: J. B. STOLLMEYER, West Indies

IN the thirties, umpiring in competitive club cricket in the West Indies was often of questionable standard, both as regards its quality and bias. As a young player presumably of promise I found occasionally that I had the umpire on my side as the following will illustrate.

I was playing for the Queen's Park Cricket Club against my old school Queen's Royal College and opened the batting. After scoring about 10 I touched one to the 'keeper but the deafening appeal was answered by an equally loud "Not out" by the umpire, who, incidentally, wore a very dark pair of eyeshades. Counting myself lucky I continued until I was hit (or so I thought) plumb in front but, as I prepared to leave, the same umpire was adamant that I was "not out". After these lucky escapes I made good progress until I entered the nervous nineties when in attempting an injudicious single I found myself run-out by a couple of yards. My friend the umpire was however to be seen solemnly shaking his head. "Not out," he said, and as I pulled up from my exertions I saw him looking benevolently at me. He could contain himself no longer. Lowering his eye-shades and winking mischievously at me, he said *sotto voce*, "Mr. Jeff, you are batting like a cat—nine lives."

From: EDDIE BARLOW, South Africa

IN a game in Johannesburg it occurred that a batsman was given out caught behind. The batsman felt he had come nowhere near touching it.

The following is the conversation that took place.

"Howzat," screamed the bowler.

The umpire upheld the appeal, "That's out."

The batsman was aghast. He couldn't believe his eyes.

Eventually he got out, "What for?"

The umpire looked rather worried at this stage but replied triumphantly:

"For the whole . . . afternoon!"

Index

Graham McKenzie, 84
Roy McLean, 88
Michael Melford, 52
Keith Miller, 69
Hanif Mohammed, 90
Clifford Mollison, 25, 26

G. C. NEWMAN, 12
Dudley Nourse (Jnr.), 54

PAT O'SHAUGHNESSY, 66

PETER PARFITT, 35
John Pawle, 8
Arthur Phebey, 62
Graeme Pollock, 90
Fred Price, 34
Jack Price, 41

JOHN REID, 87
Wilfred Rhodes, 7
Peter Richardson, 34, 53
R. C. Robertson-Glasgow, 31
Gordon Ross, 46
Sir Stanley Rous, 17

ANDREW SANDHAM, 80
M. J. K. Smith, 6

John Snagge, 77
Garfield Sobers, 82
Brian Statham, 43, 63, 64
J. B. Stollmeyer, 92
Bert Sutcliffe, 84
Herbert Sutcliffe, 60

FRED TITMUS, 7
Jack Train, 11
Freddie Trueman, 44
Frank Tyson, 41
Wynford Vaughan-Thomas, 26

JOHN WAITE, 88
Ronnie Waldman, 42
Rev. Emrys Walters, 54
John Warner, 10, 21
J. J. Warr, 33
Naunton Wayne, 30
Roy Webber, 15, 65
Peter West, 7, 44, 69
Arthur Wood, 74
John Woodcock, 50
Frank Woolley, 20, 38
D. V. P. Wright, 59
Arthur Wrigley, 18, 70
R. E. S. Wyatt, 78

NORMAN YARDLEY, 31, 72

[96]